THE END OF
THE WORLD

Daniella

Earthalujah!

Rev Billy

THE END OF THE WORLD

REVEREND BILLY

STOP SHOPPING PUBLISHING
New York

© 2012 Reverend Billy

Published by Stop Shopping Publishing

First printing 2012
This printing 2014

See last page for image permissions.

Cataloging-in-Publication data is available from the Library of Congress. A catalog record for this book is available from the British Library.

ISBN 978-0-9915298-2-7 paperback
ISBN 978-0-9915298-1-0 e-book

This book is set in the typefaces Bodoni, Klavika, New Caledonia, and Steelfish. Typeset by Bathcat Ltd.

for Savi and Lena

CONTENTS

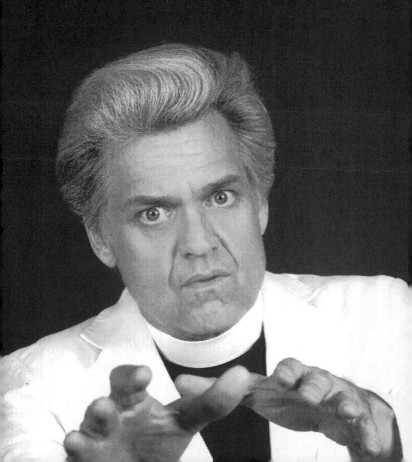

the HAPPY

ENDING

*It was a distraction, as The End of the World approached,
that there were still such great sales.*

*New and improved Apple apps, survivalist yoga
techniques, "Drowning Elmo" toys—all kinds of things.*

*The tsunamis and heat-waves and flash floods and
volcanoes and hurricanes bounced on the horizon
like Loony Tunes.*

The accelerating Apocalypse got us hot.

The really bad disasters were available on Pay-Per-View.

What didn't kill us made us watch.

We could take a mile-wide tornado off the shelf, hit a button, watch it drop into a city and wow! It was like watching Lady Gaga doing the splits in a dress made of flank steaks.

You can say one thing about the humans: we were a species that scribbled, texted, hologrammed, and burst a blood vessel of pixels in the final years of modern life.

IF THE REVOLUTION WASN'T TELEVISED THE END OF THE WORLD CERTAINLY WAS

Millions of movies were found on mounds of stinking corpses, still flickering on screens through cold grasping fingers, glowing at the bottom of sodden suitcases.

Of the six known mass extinctions on Earth, this was the self-conscious one, produced and consumed in high-def, broad-color with advanced compression algorithms.

The End of the World was the story-line of all best-selling movies and books. In its own way, this was the perfect happy ending. The media was made, completed, and shipped to consumers. The End was casually tagged "to be continued."

A kind of eternity was claimed: "Products have the power to survive and you can join them beyond the storms and fires and floods—no money down!" This sustained a certain giddiness in the culture.

But it was not a pretty sight, the day the humans went into the ditch. The bitterness had become embarrassing. Home-owners fumed at the coyotes and cockroaches that poured through the front doors of their suburban palaces as they packed their SUVs for the final drive.

The "this-isn't-fair-we've-been-betrayed-by-Nature" was a favorite kvetch, as if the new predators were going off-script. And speaking of predators why hadn't the United States of America already saved the world? The USA was supposed to be the hero. We'd seen it a thousand times. In fact some consumers thought the world WAS saved, but they were on the wrong channel.

So death was denied and dying was purchased with relish.

That old pre-apocalyptic approach to death wasn't as good for business as the disaster market, whose growth could only end when every last shopper was grotesquely, operatically dead.

Where are the consumers? Oh, the consumers consumed the consumers.

What do you do?

You stop watching. Stop shopping. You get away. How do you get away? You run across a field and keep running.

JOIN THE ANIMALS

GLOBAL
LONELINESS

CHILDREN,
IN THE CHURCH OF STOP SHOPPING
WE HAVE MADE A DISCOVERY—
THE HUMAN LAW OF CLIMATE CHANGE.
HERE IT IS:

There is a direct relationship between each additional minute that we are separated and every pound of greenhouse gas that is added to the air. The greater the distance that individual human beings are from one another, the more CO_2 we put in the air. Let me say it another way: SPLIT US APART—WE KILL. (Very lonely people make very big tornadoes.) It's not just that we are social animals. It's that when we're anti-social we are *downright deadly*.

Here's today's Apocalypse. Seven billion people have fallen out of love. We have been forced out of the House of Love by the Devil.

Our global economy, fundamentalist religion, and national security are each based on increasing the distance between us. The Federal Reserve does not want us to hang out. The distancing that is their "growth" comes in products that surround us and then separate us.

That's a problem, children.

THE GROSS NATIONAL PRODUCT NEEDS OUR LONELINESS

The built-in isolation is enforced by two things.

First: constant, disorienting motion (relationship-fracturing, job-searches, housing displacement, long distance commutes, migration from poverty, famine, or war).

Second: sensual disengagement from others, (touching replaced by pixelating, couch-potato illnesses, information stress and the modern affliction called "media loneliness," shopping and psychopathic living through perfume, cosmetic surgery and lonely liposuction, traffic jams from an abominating hell, gated communities where masturbation and adultery are the only transcendence). In one word: Consumerism.

Producers and consumers grow farther apart as sales increase. Consumers are increasingly isolated from each other. Profits create opposition and opposition creates profit. No type of consumer is ever more important than THE ENEMY.

WAR IS CRUCIAL TO CONSUMERISM

Militarism demands the largest products and the longest distribution lines. Intimacies within wars arise but they are closely monitored, bands of brothers may save each other's lives but only *after* the products have exploded.

All the Apocalypses in this book come from separation. The more terrible The End of the World, the clearer the call to look into each other's eyes and start something. Earth in me recognizes Earth in you. The Earth wants to reunite.

the END *of*

BIRTH

Death is one thing,
an end to birth is something else.

—MICHAEL SOULÉ AND BRUCE WILCOX

Tropical forests, wetlands, estuaries, and the coral reefs beneath the ocean's surface are the home ecosystems for most of the life on Earth.

Tropical forests are the home of half of all species, and they are, as of the beginning of 2012, one-third gone. Caught in the slash-and-burn lumbering, fast-food grazing, and accelerating birthrates, the planet will be deforested for our children.

We are turning out the lights on the creation of life. Life needs enough life—forests and oceans of it—to keep making life. Life-a-lujah! Put it this way: evolution, to work, needs its genetic pool, its laboratory, its *wildness*.

Human beings are making this declaration: "With *our* creation—evolution is complete. Nature got us going, but now it's final destiny-time! Push that throttle! On to Greatness!" Well, that greatness could be over in a few days . . .

America is addicted to the future. Our culture has hundreds of

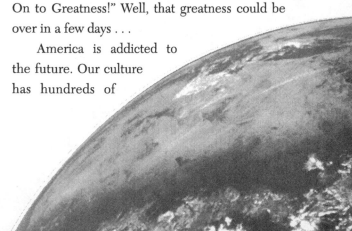

expensive think tanks dedicated to considering the future. The prevailing American thoughts on the matter swerve into bad science fiction. The plan seems to be: The people will wait at a bus-stop for the Second Coming. Whatever our future, our glorious beaming-up leaves us an isolated species.

In fact, the survival of any life depends on other life. Even the most basic inanimate elements of the planet—gasses and temperatures, fluids and minerals —cannot exist independent of living organisms.

In the early nineties, Mr. Ed Bass, from a Texas oil family, financed an experiment in which minia-tures of some of Earth's ecosystems were sequestered with a group of scientists inside a glass bubble called Biosphere 2 near Tuscon, Arizona. They housed a coral reef in one wing, with pumps cycling salt-water. There was a rainforest in another wing, and so on. They introduced a few lizards and insects but no mammals or birds— membership in this club anticipated a mostly human Earth. Space colonization was mentioned in early press releases as a motive for the hermetically-sealed experiments. A comedy of bad science loomed over the project even before the scientists started sneaking out for chocolate bars.

Inside the bubble they couldn't get the trees to stand up straight. They caressed the bark. The trees drooped sadly. They discovered that trees need wind. They get their strength from swaying in the breeze. So they tried fanning the trees inside their expensive terrarium, but the trees just leaned and leaned. *Trees need wind.*

It was recently discovered that 45% of the CO_2 stored on land is inside trees. So the wind makes a tree into a tree, and the tree also makes the wind into wind, by cleaning it, scrubbing the carbon, and returning the oxygen over and over. Wind needs trees. Trees need wind.

Humans needs both.

We are witnessing the extinction of hundreds of thousands of species of life: birds, mammals, frogs and lizards and bees and butterflies, woody plants and flowers . . . we select some to save, conserve, preserve. We make them into media stars and treasure them, but this planet is our greenhouse now and we don't plan on sharing it much. The ongoing and upcoming extinction wave seems to leave us officially unimpressed. The candidates at their debates, with their audience of 70 million, couldn't bring themselves to say the word Climate, or even the word Earth.

THIS IS AN APOCALYPSE OF ACCUMULATING SILENCE

The idea that we would remain the only living thing—with Earth repurposed to include only pets, little micro climate samples preserved like pocket parks, a rainforest the size of a par 3 golf hole, and museums full of extinct-in-the-wilds animals staring back at us in wonder. That's Hell, but at least it's a temporary one, since we would not survive long.

Who would say openly that human beings are the only life worth saving? It seems so absurd. And yet that seems to be the plan. The most basic and far-reaching policy of the United States leadership at this time is to *do nothing, say nothing, and change nothing.*

In this slow motion orgy of death, we go about our day with the understanding that life as we know it is ending. We go to work (if we can find it), raise our kids (if we can find them), have sex (if we can get it), sleep and wake up. We know it won't be long.

THE GLOBAL GOING-CRAZY TIPPING POINT

ZOMBIE NO GO GO, UNLESS YOU TELL AM TO GO

ZOMBIE NO GO STOP, UNLESS YOU TELL AM TO STOP

ZOMBIE NO GO TURN, UNLESS YOU TELL AM TO TURN

ZOMBIE NO GO THINK, UNLESS YOU TELL AM TO THINK

—FELA KUTI, "ZOMBIE, ZOMBIE"

Something broad and deep about human nature is deleted now. That evolution instruction *"Fight or Flight!"* is reversed into *"Stop and Shop!"* This is the End of the World as a White Hot 2-Day Sale at Best Buy!

Did someone say that reports of the Earth's death are greatly exaggerated? In June 2012 a study called "Approaching A State Shift In Earth's Biosphere," from an international group of 22 natural scientists, systems theorists, and climatologists was published in the journal Nature. The report's lead author was Dr. Tony Barnosky from UC-Berkeley. It came out after the record 109 tornadoes in North America in May, and just before the hottest July ever recorded.

The scientists asked: Could the life of the entire Earth be a single ecosystem? Could it collapse all at once like smaller ecosystems have, like the North Atlantic fisheries, or the aspen forests in the Rockies?

The report is a premonition, a brave gaze across the border into planetary Armageddon. Read this paragraph carefully. If you're shopping you might not notice The End of the World.

> *Rapid climate change combined with highly fragmented species ranges can be expected to magnify the potential for ecosystem collapse, and wholesale landscape changes may in turn influence the biology of oceans.*

And later in this Mother of all Apocalypses:

> *The global ecosystem . . . is approaching a planetary-scale critical transition as a result of human influence. Humans are now facing the potential to transform Earth rapidly and irreversibly into a state unknown in human experience.*

Now children—maybe I'm a shopper like most of my country. Maybe I'm waiting in line like a zombie. But I sense a predator in these warning words. My reptilian brain is flickering, what are those reflections on the shiny gossip magazines? The shadow is falling toward me fast. The heavy hot furry weight is on me and there is a great jaw around my neck. Help! I'm gonna turn and fight for my life! I'll throw this Golden Dawn detergent at the tiger of Climate Change!

The Barnosky study is as grave a warning as I have ever read. Yet these natural scientists are so isolated from mainstream culture that no one much noticed it. No parallel professional class will take up The End of the World, even with the combined testimony of these 22 illustrious researchers. For one thing, scientists have no Carl Sagan now, no Stephen Jay Gould, no Rachel Carson or Wangari Maathi or Aldo Leopold or Edward Abbey. The great planet-criers are gone. Do we have a living counterpart?

This is a time of widespread distortion. Unless we have a blast of honesty from Wikileaks or Ai WeiWei—the world is just seeing things. What a strange echo-chamber we live in. Beyonce has a billion hits. There are clouds above us full of songs and jokes. But, how do we talk about the weather? We are standing in line, silently, there with our soap.

Elizabeth Hadly of Stanford, one of the Barnosky study's authors, added some warm-blooded remarks:

> We may already be past these tipping points in particular regions of the world. I just returned from a trip to the high Himalayas in Nepal, where I witnessed families fighting each other with machetes for wood—wood that they would burn to cook their food in one evening. In places where governments are lacking basic infrastructure, people fend for themselves, and biodiversity suffers. We desperately need global leadership for planet Earth.

Global leadership? You mean Obama and Hillary Clinton at the Copenhagen climate conference three years ago? What did they do with that historic opportunity? Show-off shoot-em-ups with China, India, and Brazil. Some photo-opping and a little duty-free shopping and they fled in their jet.

Children—This kind of scary study usually pops up in newspapers as a little squib on page 8. I always look for the sentence that calms me down, something along the lines of "Sea-rise, population pressures, and mass migrations from coastal cities will peak by the end of the century." It's that first phrase that I look for, with its promise to hold off destruction till 2100. That 80-or-90-year gift would give Lena a life.

In the last year or so I have been unable to find the "end of the century" phrase. Barnosky's team is eerily silent on the question, but each sentence seems to scream THE END IS NEAR!

There is *"Fight or Flight!"* There is *"Stop and Shop!"* And then there is *"Going Crazy!"* I'm wondering about mass schizophrenia, as the sky worsens, as the ground shakes, as the fires and floods make their way toward us?

We are zombies no go go, unless you tell us to go. We're consumers standing in line. We are told to stay in line, promised a steady product-drip of orgasm-lite if we buy and buy. If we are zombified, then who inherits the old get-up-and-go of active humanity? The Corporation. The Market. This is crazy-making.

Let us now damn famous money. It is bonkers that the leading players in the life of Earth are these corporate cults, with logos and slogans and budgets bigger than countries. Our national leaders are corporate spokespersons: green-washing pours from their mouths. But the sympathetic traits of the hero go to giant blocks of money shot this way and that by thousands of suits at computers. "The market is nervous today." "Investors are in the pink, after good earnings reports in China." "Corporations are waiting as the Euro hesitates."

Yes, the old pluck of the survivor has transferred to corporations. They have got us so involved in the outcome of their touching story that Black Friday grosses are actually presented as the emotional climax of the year. Corporations fight through the hard times with the language once reserved for pioneer families on the Oregon Trail. Oh yes, corporations have endless resiliency. They will bounce back forever.

Of course, the corporate market is people, you and I, and we don't bounce back forever.

THE TIGER WILL RIP OUT OUR NECK EXACTLY ONCE

Roughly 400,000 people have already died in climate disasters in the last 12 months. They are dead, and off the market.

Where are you? Children, are you walking through the air that is 50 degrees wrong? Are you walking under the tampered sky in the 10th year of no rain?

We are millions trying to get dressed and go to work as screams travel back and forth inside our bodies, as our own shock and disbelief pulls on our faces. We push in the ear-buds, Adele sings "Rolling in the Deep."

When did our lives start drifting up a fluorescent aisle of dazzling products? The corporations study us from their surveillance cameras and they see that we still remember this thing called Earth.

Sometimes our suspicions are aroused. Was that fire supposed to be the size of France? The investigators see that we have Earth in our eyes. That we know—we are the main predator. We ourselves are the internal workings of that tiger, as we buy our Golden Dawn. Then the corporations hold their breath. Will we turn on them? Will we break from our line inside the beast, and try to live?

They watch us as we leave the store with our shopping bag and walk to the bus-stop, making a concerted effort not to buckle over in sobs and fucking-fuck rants.

THIS IS THE DARK WEIGHT OF KILLING OURSELVES IN PUBLIC

We are falling together. The slaughter with the perfect cover. Each of us is absorbing this tragedy personally. It is the best-kept Apocalypse.

Yes, I'm crazy. My city is crazy. My species is crazy. The human soap opera makes no sense at all. And nobody can talk about it. That's what is surprising me. This is the Information Age, but some subjects are prurient, like our survival.

These days are deadly and funny. The comedians are less hilarious than my daughter and the tragedians not nearly as dark as the leaders who make excuses for squandered life.

The
NEW YORK
of the
EARTH
is EARTH

I'm standing in our doorway at dusk, looking out at the branches strewn up and down the street, hanging over the edges of the roofs. They look like imploring arms, like veins of dark lightning. With me is our 2-year-old Lena. She hugs my leg and catches my eye with a look from the center of the world.

I live in New York City with my partner Savitri and our Lena. We have our place, near Prospect Park. There are 20 million people around here and some of us are in terrible torment. Regardless of what we're doing— we all have the storming going on inside us a week later. It is a strange feeling that our city was swallowed by something so dark and huge, with the name of a 50's teenager. The way the house groaned and whistled—I can still feel it. Lena? You seem to have moved on.

For decades the storm battering NYC was Consumerism. The mono-culture—malls and chains and deluxe condos—flooded down into New York's key living organisms, our 500 distinct neighborhoods. Tens of thousands of family businesses and complex laughing and dancing societies on street corners, were drowned in the Sea of Identical Details. We lost our soul to an invasive species.

Lena coos and laughs, pushing on my arms. Oh you are a little alluvial drumlin of a girl, an interglacial toddler. And Lena is a New Yorker. And we can't see a single logo from our front door. This is the way to raise a child! Logo-free!

Look at all the branches and twigs, Lena! The ripped-off and crashed tree limbs are everywhere, like death-grabs along the pavement. Is Sandy against the Demon Mono-culture? Will the giving and loving in Coney and Rockaway—will it rise against the Brands on higher ground? Sandy cracks the right angles, spirals the straight lines, shorts the wires . . . and we're left kinder for it. Sandy might be just what the Apple needs.

Suddenly, my neighbor's head makes an appearance, a violation of our scenic view.

"Good evening Billy! . . . How is Lena tonight?"

"Hello . . . Oh, Lena is . . . Lena is in a good mood but I don't know why."

"I know why. I'm in the same mood for the same reason."

"Oh? And what mood is that?"

My neighbor is so nice. How can I resist? . . . so pleasant. Her eyes are glinting like sunlight on a lake. Her name is Pam. She says, "Oh I don't know . . . It's the happy mood of . . . I survived, that's all."

We look out at the twilight a minute. The wind sounds like difficult breathing. Is this still Sandy? Pam pipes up, "Yeah, we're in trouble. Listen Billy, I got food on the stove—see you . . . Bye Lena."

Wait a minute. I love New York. When I was a kid in South Dakota I used to go out at night and I would gaze up at satellites moving between the stars and I would dream that Manhattan was a great ship sailing through the dark, piloted by Duke Ellington and Leonard Bernstein.

I love New York. I bought into this place. I'm Broadway, failing to mention Earth for hundreds of consecutive million-dollar plays. I'm the media and art machine, career-addicted at precisely the point that careers don't matter. I'm a Marxist birdwatcher. I'm a green billionaire mayor who doesn't recycle. I'm New York's Finest. I put people who act wrong in The Tombs because I work for the big banks . . . And I'm a New York chauvinist and it's up to you New York, New York.

And I'm suffering some remorse, as the dazzle dims, as the backwater pours in, as the ocean fills Wall Street's basements.

The assumption was that Sandy was impossible, because nature only comes here in sex, death and the Bronx Zoo. We didn't build levees because—how could a storm stop the Apple?

The capital of world culture is not New York City. It's Earth. It is the entire wet green and blue rock, that's the center, the whole spinning rock with all its magical life, which gave us Lena. Now she's picking mint out of a crack in the sidewalk.

APOCALYPSE

of the

FORESTS

Right now there is a broad forest mortality sweeping through Africa, Australia, Russia, the entire western US, from BC through the Rockies and Sierras to New Mexico . . . whole mountain ranges are covered with dead trees. The forests are dying.

All the known causes can be traced to climate change: warming, drought, bark-beetles, and wild-fire. International teams of scientists are coming in with the first world-wide forest reviews. Dr. Craig Allen from the US Geological Survey at Los Alamos gathered reports by 19 natural scientists who specialize in forest life of every kind: savannas, conifers, Mediterranean woodlands, temperate evergreen and deciduous forests, and evergreen broadleaved tropical forests. Every scientist reports general wide-spread mortality of their forests in the last 36 months.

The forestry scientists feel the full gravity of what is happening. They know intimately about this global phenomenon of death. Talking with a tree scientist from New Mexico while researching this book, I hear a voice both sad and incredulous. She remembers the hard work of trying to wake up the public over clear-cut lumbering in the Pacific Northwest, especially of the Redwoods, and doubts the issue of all the forests dying can gain the public's attention. She talks candidly about the passing of the forests.

There is no Save The Panda anymore. No sad, cuddly face that you can sell to the plastic-swiping middle classes of the West. No noble wolf with the howling silhouette. Not anymore. The era of the dying species as media star is passing. Now it is whole ecosystems are disappearing, countless species all at once. Now it is forests, dying forests.

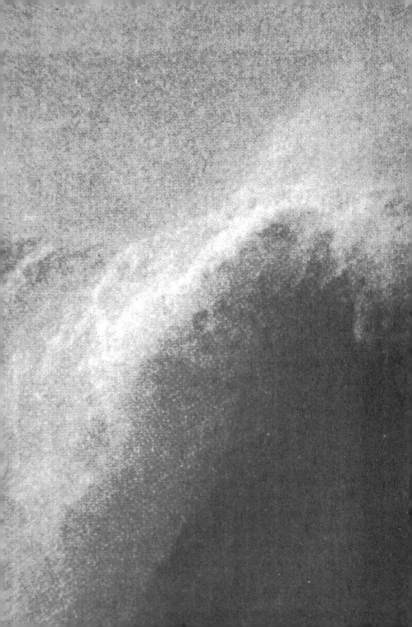

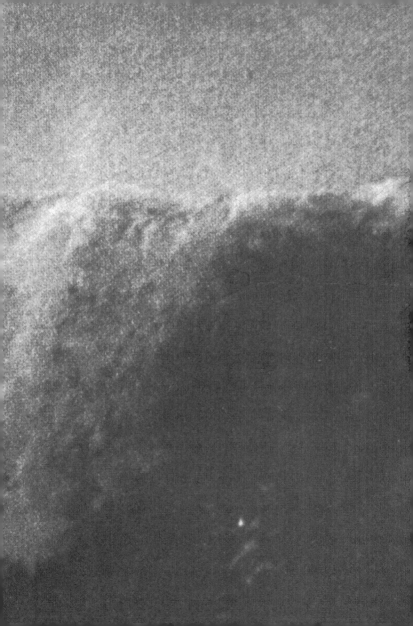

OLD
TREES

From so long ago that I can't remember, from before I could walk or talk—I was aware that at the end of my grandparents' back lawn there were towering old pine trees. They were the front edge of wildness, beyond them was the forest. Those trees had me spellbound all through my childhood. The branches were like black longboats floating in the sky.

One day, when I was about 6 or 7, I was walking away from the house across the grass toward the trees. I walked by the midway point of the yard, with the little arch of roses that marked as far as I was allowed to go. But I kept going, into the second half of the lawn, stretching toward the roots of the huge old trees. I felt sort of dizzy out there, walking too far, and then I looked up at those branches. It was late in the day—a deep red flaming sunset was coloring everything in different ways.

I stopped. It seemed to me that the pine trees were watching the sunset. That's what it felt like. A chill went through me.

I was in the early grades. So I was reading children's books with cats and pigs that had opinions and mountains that had bad moods. In my child's world a big tree could have feelings, certainly. But this was something different. These were not loveable, humanized animals talking to each other, teaching numbers and letters. I felt that time itself was standing at attention inside the trees, old giants who knew about life and death and loved the beauty of a day passing into night.

A tree is a living thing. We think of a tree's consciousness as authoritative and wise and mysterious. We have sustained much of our human poetry with meditations on arboreal splendor.

Our love of forests doesn't keep us from destroying them. We have killed trees like no other living thing. So we better break out of that old sentimentality and create a Forest Faith that makes action possible.

The End of the World answers the question "What will it take to survive?" with the answer "Whatever it takes, hurry up." Anne and Paul Ehrlich, authors of the *The Population Bomb*, mused on what it would take to avert disaster:

> *Scientific analysis points, curiously, toward the need for a quasi-religious transformation of contemporary cultures.*

So what would a Forest Faith look like? Let's take this on in our clumsy Western way. We're in counter-intuitive territory here.

Say that trees don't die in the way that we imagine

death. Imagine that they decompose, are eaten by fire or bark-beetles, by moss and fungi, their ashen molecules pulled into the air by the wind, into the water by rivers and down to the sea, and then up into the cycle of evaporation and precipitation and back down and around and around.

Imagine that nothing is destroyed finally. What was always here is still here. Imagine that the trees fly into the wind and the water and retain their treeness, their forestness, even as they disintegrate into ever smaller bits of wood.

Is this a curious quasi semi-religious regard for the eternity of the tree's life? I'm a modern man stumbling toward what the old cultures always knew. Yes, imagine that the trees go up into the great circles of water and lightning bolts and high winds that travel from an individual tree's death up into the defiance of gravity and the creation of a raging storm, a super storm, a Climate Change storm.

Climate Change. It's a very staid little phrase, isn't it? Doesn't seem so deadly. The phrase itself seems afraid of its own implications. But what could be in that change?

Modern science will find out what the storms are really made of some day. Now they are made of our mathematics, of vectors and humidity, and causes and effects that we can measure. Our Forest Faith believes that the storms are full of lives that have been lived long ago. Sandy grew to a thousand miles wide and turned left to enter the big city like the vengeful resurrection of the world's dead trees. In our Forest Faith we believe that there are forests inside the storms!

The writhing beauty of the roots, the pulsing smiles under the bark pushing water up into the leaves where the green miracle of photosynthesis takes place, the gentle raking of the sky's invisible gasses—all of this is inside the storm that rips off our roofs. We have to imagine that life is there.

A STORM IS A LIVING THING

It may be a nightmare for us, it may cause great sorrow and suffering for us, but it has its own apoc-alyptic ecstatic life that we can't see. The storm, we in the Forest Faith believe, is having its fit of remembering. It is a great, dark cloud, a 1,000 mile churning cloud—remembering the forests full of thrashing trees that long for the lives they lived on the land below.

Oh, these unprecedented climate change storms! Are they full of unappeased forests flying toward their new seed?

Imagine that!

POST-SCRIPT

Treehugger!

I can feel my congregation squirming in the pews. Making up a shake-and-bake faith—it's foolishness, isn't it?

Our Forest Faith, where trees have souls: This idea asks us to imagine life where we assumed there was only a paved bald treeless planet. This all comes out of Sandy. We watched the sky trying to re-forest miles of high-stress concrete. And where there were forests— well the trees flew across town.

The sadness of the passing of forests is deeper than the blues. The commons of our cities are shadows of the clearings of forests. We surround ourselves with forest-shapes because we came from them—spires and curving walls and tall windows. In New York there are forest satyrs gazing from the cornices of buildings . . .

Now here is religious instruction for you. Amen? After our service today seek out a tree. Say hello, ask the tree for permission to touch it—and let yourself embrace that tree with your whole body. To quote a sexy anthem—"Don't let go!" Hug that tree, children, until it whispers a sweet nothing in your mind. Until it has a personality. A tree-onality. Now that's embarrassing. Feel the cynicism coming up? Don't let go. This is important. Put your ear in the bark and listen.

To save our own lives we have to save the tree's life. That means: we must remember that this tree is a life. Then we might get back on track saving our own lives.

We've never changed anything in our country without risking our own lives to save others' lives. That's how we've always done it. Consumerism tries to stop us— but that's our basic move.

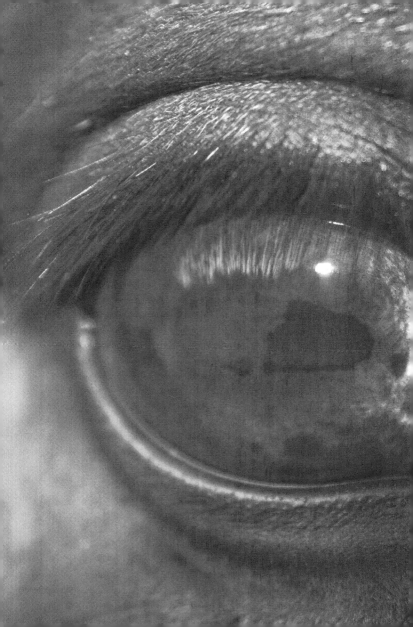

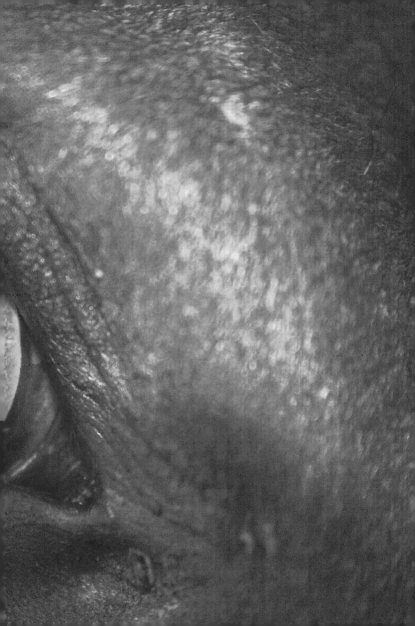

EARTH MANIFESTO

Earth is our government. Earth is our god.

Earth is our economy. Earth is our church.

*We listen to Earth and then we go back to the old
institutions.*

*We go to the president and the generals and holy fathers
and doctors of thinking —*

And we get no response.

Then we return to Earth and await further instructions,

We know that life itself is the best strategist.

Earth speaks to us every day.

The disasters are hard lessons.

The silence of extinct life is a sorrowing Earth.

What Earth knows is almost entirely unknown to us.

The unknowable Earth is everything that we believe.

It is all the commandments.

It is common sense.

It is where compassion comes from.

We put personalities on Mount Olympus to represent it.

We pray to the watery fire that creates a child in our loved one.

We make giant stone heads that stare out across the sea.

We dance all night.

Now Earth is our only celebrity.

Earth is the only famous being that matters at all.

Human history was made triumphing over Earth.

Now Earth makes history.

RESURRECTION

from the

TOMBS

I'm in jail. And oh that feeling, that sinking, shrinking feeling of the first moments of being in the Tombs, a city block below the municipal courts of New York City. It is November, cold and crowded and it stinks down here, but this time my arrest is with the people of Occupy Wall Street (OWS), and it feels different.

There are about a dozen of us, the male part of the group that locked arms and sat down at the front door of Goldman Sachs. Led by Cornel West and Chris Hedges, we marched from a people's trial in Zuccotti Park where, with an examination of the record, our judges ruled that the vampire squids pay a preliminary $87 billion fine, a judgment that we presented at the front door of Goldman Sachs' glassy, giant building at 200 West Street, just by Ground Zero and its clouds of tourists.

In our group taking the hit are Ecuadorians and Filipinos and Jews and Hindus but we descend the steps into the thousands of African-American and Hispanic-American males in the racist prison system of New York. I'm in my polyester white suit with the big hair—an Elvis impersonator in the Tombs. "So what's your church, father?" "The Church Of Stop Shopping." "STOP SHOPPING? HAH!" Then, laughter and hip hop rhymes burst out from the cells down the yellow fluorescent hallway.

The young activists of OWS are cool customers. They've been in the Tombs many times since they occupied Zuccotti Park on September 17, 2011, and they know they will be returning to their great public experiment upstairs in a few hours or days. Zuccotti Park aka Liberty Square, waits, full of people from everywhere and surrounded by an army of blue, only a couple blocks from the courts in the strangely small and tidy stage set of lower Gotham. The Occupy people can't wait to get back to their revolution, and in fact they don't wait. They start a General Assembly right there behind bars.

The cells of the Tombs are notoriously crowded, the four or five Occupy people who want to start this discussion are jailed with 40 prisoners slouching around them in the cell. There are men on the ground, crowded off the benches along the walls. They sleep balled up on the floor in their jackets, or using each others' legs as pillows.

In the Tombs you lose your relationship to the time of day and people are always sleeping while others yell—screaming at the cops for their meds or a phone call or something. In this crush of bodies and voices the General Assembly is about to commence.

These unasked-for democratic leaders are young, in their mid-twenties. They decide to squeeze through the men and stand near enough to the bars that border the neighboring cells up and down the jail hallway—thinking they can be seen from this position by more prisoners and heard by many more. So with those grimy steel bars in their faces they begin to create an agenda and a "stack" of people ready to talk, and here come the by-now-famous hand gestures of direct democracy. They have to teach the semaphore signals from scratch to their disbelieving audience.

At first I feel an excruciating awkwardness. Here? Now? But they don't hesitate, methodically teaching the prisoners the hand-signs of the GA. The cells are soon full of what looks like a clumsy tai chi class. "This is the signal that you agree with what you've just heard." "This is how you disagree." "This is 'hurry up you made your point.'" Part of my discomfort is that I consider some of these prisoners to be premier communicators of the street, and the remedial class in democratic sign language feels so sort of Mr. Rogers. It's like teaching the kazoo to Charley Parker. However, our young teachers are undeterred and soon "MIC CHECK! MIC CHECK!" fills the Tombs, startling the guards, who get up from their desks. The Tombs General Assembly is called to order.

The first item of discussion is, "Who has put us in jail? Who do the police work for?" That is an easy one. The 1% gets our world-weary vote, and the 1% is translated into crude shouts of "Boss," "Massa," and a trail of epithets that could give Jamie Dimon nightmares. This is followed by a series of decisions about the justice system in this country. A resolution passes with the wiggling upward fingers—that we reach out to the police and try to teach peaceful co-existence to the majority of them, while identifying those who are clearly too violent to remain on the job, especially when carrying a gun. Many of us presumed innocents in the Tombs that night were injured from our arrests, whether cuts, concussions, sprains, bruises, or nerve damage. That last one is my particular problem—half my right hand is numbed from the zip-loc handcuffs. Still, a vote passes that as society's change begins, we will continue to employ the judges and clerks and police in the justice industry who have families. That leaves some of the prisoners with the sensation of forgiveness, which they seem surprised by.

As I watch this underground parliament with its strange mix of innocence and sophistication, I know that there is one big vote that we have all made, that is: we are here but we are free. We are here in a jail and we are free. We are free of these walls, and this city block of earth and pavement, and these heavy cages that weigh down on us. We know that the smelly claustrophobic place we are in is meant to overwhelm us with the inevitability of this kind of justice. The statement here is that this system will go on forever. We disagree.

WE ARE FREE TO PLAN THE FUTURE OF OUR WORLD

We feel the beginning of an irresistible folk story. Dozens of police sit in silence as the ragged congress proceeds, its participants absorbing the story, preparing their comments. Like a seed from way down in the soil, this will be carried and embellished up through all the corporate censorship that looms above us.

The young men shouting "MIC CHECK!" between the bars seem to glow. The claustrophobic gravity of the Tombs bursts open. The bars disappear. The prisoners crane their necks to stay in the conversation, and even a couple cops can be seen working their fingers in the air, trying to get the language of democracy right.

1%! THIS IS THE END OF YOUR WORLD!

RITUAL GRATITUDE

and the

ROBOTS *of* DEATH

Somehow, in the last days of OWS' life in the park, a week or so after the eviction by the Wall Street army, the Zuccotti kitchen was able to cook a turkey dinner and deliver it by bicycle to a group of us who were occupying the Bank of America at Houston and Lafayette. We were thankful for that.

We looked for a gesture to tell the story. In American culture you need the Bible story, the parable, the image of the sling-shot David, of Gandhi marching to the sea, of Emma Goldman and the NYC general strike of 1909, of Dr. King on Pettis Bridge.

And so: you've seen Daniel-in-the-Lion's-Den. You smelled Jonah-in-the-Whale. And now, ladies and gents, let's give a warm welcome to:

THANKSGIVING AT THE BANK OF AMERICA!

The Thanksgiving dinner is served inside the blood red walls and silent cash machine robots of the Bank of America lobby. We carry in our food—a small parade from a nearby alley with our dinner props in the hands of the Picture the Homeless and Stop Shopping Church communities. With no security except the ever-present surveillance cameras, we enter the lobby and begin to decorate the place with tables, doilies, crystal, flowers, and even pictures on the walls—among them family scenes by Norman Rockwell.

With the layering of the family theater of Thanksgiving over the red plastic and glass environment of the bank's lobby, we feel the reversion back to the era of good feeling that bank marketing still attempts around the edges, happy actors and gleaming graphics . . . and looking around for cops, we begin to eat, while the choir quietly hums harmonies and sways, standing between the table and the ATM machines. The act of eating has an immediate and mysterious effect—it calms and humors us.

At the table, in the Jesus Christ position, is our guest of honor—Ms. Kendall Jackman!—recently evicted illegally by Bank of America's foreclosure mills. The regal Harlem mother feasts solemnly on turkey while we sing. Then she tells her story. We listen to the description of the fine print and the smiling mortgage agent two and a half years before. It is an important fact that even as Kendall went into the shelter system, her apartment remained empty.

One of the pictures we put up on the wall is a lithograph by Kurt Vonnegut, our old mentor—a sneaky departure from the Life Magazine decor. We brought it for good luck, "The Three Magi from the View of the Christ Child"—six eyes floating in a tangle of orbs and curves. Father Kurt!

We recreate the ambience of Kendall's home, like so many destroyed by this criminal bank, in the red lobby. The robotic cash machines stand stolidly by, unable to stop us. During the meal, police drive by and wave. The Thanksgiving ritual has its own power, and creates a kind of micro-government, encouraging bank customers to walk through our dining room respectfully.

With such a devil as Bank of America, we are able to protest environmental and social justice at one and the same time. The bank that illegally evicts the most people is also among the top investors in Dirty Coal. So the destruction of the family home is equated with the destruction of the large home of Earth.

We made media from our Thanksgiving—videos and photographs. We wondered if we were on the right track. Activism that goes to the oldest, homespun rituals . . . yes there is surprising power there, as unlikely as it might for an activist. The arrangement of loving, the conscious creation of a family memory at that old meal—has the seed of revolution in it. Gratitude and the gift. The gift and gratitude. Back and forth. It is the seed that would undermine the market that evicted Kendall and millions of American families.

Enacting our own Thanksgiving, feeling the honest slowed-down emotions come up in us during our ritual meal—got an essential no-nonsense going inside the discombobulating holiday bullshit of Bank of America's lobby graphics. The famous fraudster can't foreclose actual gratitude and giving.

I was able to say in my brief remarks, earning a "Praise Be!" from Kendall and our choir and the robot buck-suckers—that banks must become public now.

APOCALYPSE *of*

the
MOUNTAINTOPS

THERE ARE ABOUT 80 OF US, Savitri and myself and an eclectic group of Europeans, South Americans, and Russians.

First, we gather in the courtyard of Barcelona's Museum of Contemporary Art. Amen? Savitri announces that the name of our action is "Naked Grief," and that we will have to learn how to cry energetically —with tears all the better!—in public. We'll do this in Deutsche Bank—a bank that finances CO_2 emissions. As we sob and moan, we will remove our clothing. Then we will rub ourselves with coal and cry even harder.

So we practice crying in that courtyard. Savitri coaches us in our exercises in public wailing. It is easy for a few seconds, but out-and-out crying, sobbing, retching, really sorrowing for ten minutes? It is hard to do. We have to start crying over and over again.

To help the people who are having trouble crying on purpose, we go down into the politics of this act. Deutsche Bank is among the banks that finance Mountaintop Removal (MTR). Do you want to cry? Imagine a mountain in Appalachia. The coal company inserts dynamite into deep holes, then lifts the whole ecosystem into the air to die. The cries of surprise and pain range across the mountain. Nests fall from trees, deer try to run but catapult dead through the air, the creatures on the forest floor are crushed, the mountain is uprooted and broken. Then bulldozers with wheels 40 feet high begin to push the dead "over-burden" into the neighboring valley, into the pristine mountain streams below, where the fish lay their eggs and the delicate frogs sing courtship songs. Where Mountain Laurel drops its petals and ferns grow from hundred year old beds of moss.

Do you want to cry? MTR is a highly profitable but deadly coal-mining practice. Long sequestered chemicals like selenium, arsenic, and mercury float down wind, cancer clusters along their flight path. Toxins seep into the water table . . . it goes on and on. Do you want to cry?

Yes, we cry, and with ever more feeling, until we are ready to walk to the bank. Savitri leads us in her tan trenchcoat. We walk through the narrow streets of the old city, full to bursting with mopeds and bikes and our throng. When we get to the Deutsche Bank I hold the door open and Savitri walks out of her coat, emerging all white skin and freckles and dark red hair. We are weeping. People disrobe to varying degrees. We are extremely naked, for a German bank.

The inconsolable wailing has a strange power. Among us are many Spanish folk who know all about cante jon-do. They can hurl down the betrayal of the heart like no rightwing televangelist ever could. The bank managers who walk down to the first floor to see what all the trouble is about are

STARTLED BY THE POWER OF THE CRYING

The naked form of Savitri hits them harder than good graphics. The earth goddess turned banshee debt-killer is lifting an imploring arm to the fluorescent lighting. I'm shouting all the sins of big banks, blood-curdling the research. Preaching the CO_2 emissions. The mountains. A good shout for every animal.

We start crushing coal over Savitri's white skin, as tears pour down her face. Somewhere in the bank the money suddenly becomes real. The investments are full of cries and death. The bulldozer pushes against the stunned life. I lose my voice.

Getting down to the root and stem of an emotion— the wailing of "Naked Grief" opens up space that is no longer consumerized. The pictures of happy customers (played by actors trained at contentment) on the bank's walls are suddenly inconsequential. The naked and grieving foreground is irresistible. Hundreds of curious citizens along the edges of the action read the info sheets we give them, then look up again, checking the flesh. When the crying finally stops, it feels like the Peaceable Kingdom. Raw uncorporatized experience returns! An emotion in a public place, a human being crying in a bank lobby. Now why is that so powerful?

We discovered in Zuccotti that living ordinary life in public is a far-reaching and impactful protest form. I should say that we *re-discovered* that impactful protest form, since all American social change was attended by the shared pursuit of daily life, food, shelter, knowledge. People making community is a clarifying drama, a surprising prosecution of the lie that corporations foist on us—that they are normal, and that their spaces are just like our spaces and how we act in their spaces is the natural way to act in all spaces. The gravity and intensity of actual living has the effect of revealing their theft of our lives.

The corporations showered the simple gestures of living with exaggerated indictments, beginning with criminal trespass. In Zuccotti and thousands of occupied commons, the sharing of food, media, schooling, music, medicine—was encircled by armadas of Darth Vaders with guns. JP Morgan Chase gave the cops five million dollars directly, and the arsenals of fear spiraled. But they were right to panic. Something uncontrolled—the human ecosystem! Survival! . . . can begin from a bit of unadorned real life, showing itself in public.

We searched for many years for a form that protest would take, and it was hiding in plain sight. For decades we carried on with '60s style rallies and marches, and felt the lack of impact, the shrug of onlookers, the derision in the press. But the doing of life and living in public? That's it! We're on to something here!

LIFE!
LIFE-A-LUJAH!

In Barcelona we went a step further. We made a community, we expressed ourselves as a community, we mourned together, and the power of that dead mountain's life entered the self-anointed holy lobby of the Deutsche Bank. As removed and cleanly polished of any Earth as the bank is, the life of the mountains that died at its hands came up through the naked bodies of crying activists.

EARTHALUJAH!

I GOT TO BE
IMPOSSIBLE

I see Peace hit the talking
heads like amazing facial tics.
I see Orangutans debating the
mahogany loggers.
I got to be surreal sometimes
to understand.

I see the plain truth rising like
a '50s Japanese lizard.
I see rec rooms devour Rupert
Murdoch in front of his sons.
I got to be exorcized sometimes
to understand.

I see new drug laws that give
prosecutors no time to play with.
I see the fine print open like
a prison door.
I got to be impossible sometimes
to understand.

I GOT TO BE SURREAL.
I GOT TO BE EXORCISED.
I GOT TO BE IMPOSSIBLE
SOMETIMES TO UNDERSTAND.

You see the Starbucks Mermaid
got her nipples back.
You see fake bohemianism
swallowed by your sidewalks.

You got to be surreal sometimes
to understand.

You see the stock exchange
paying for itself for once.
You see the CEO cannot cash
his welfare check.
You got to be impossible sometimes
to understand.

You see tourists walk backwards
out of their pollution.
You see them go home and
demand a local paradise.
You got to be exorcised sometimes
to understand.

I GOT TO BE SURREAL.
I GOT TO BE EXORCISED.
I GOT TO BE IMPOSSIBLE
SOMETIMES TO UNDERSTAND.

We see Goofy and Jimmy Swaggart
down in the OK Corral.
We see the battle of the
disastrous religions.
We got to be surreal sometimes
to understand.

We see the Pentagon wake up
from its video game.
We see the whistling shrapnel
is not pixelated.

We got to be exorcised sometimes
to understand.

We see Teleprompter loves the
President like a Praying Mantis.
We see the Oval Office is hatching
litters of flying White Rhinos.
We got to be impossible sometimes
to understand.

WE GOT TO BE SURREAL.
WE GOT TO BE EXORCISED.
WE GOT TO BE IMPOSSIBLE
SOMETIMES TO UNDERSTAND.

Earth
Riots

EARTH RIOTS RAGED YESTERDAY,
as thousands of tree people crossed the Hudson,
establishing beach-heads along the Westside Highway,
planting trees, and then disappearing in the Green-
wich Village area, apparently taken in by sympathetic
local residents. Police are trying to keep the so-called
"Earthers" from reaching crowds of animal-humans
who occupy the Great Meadow in Central Park.

Meanwhile bird people were observed by police
landing in Bronx, and west from the Far Rockaways
in Brooklyn. The mayor asked that the administration
in Washington declare, "The Earthers are terrorists.
Parents need to keep their children home. Birds and
fish and trees should not be invited into our homes . . ."

The tornado-laden storms that have hovered over
New Jersey in recent years seemed to give the fish people
cover. They seized Liberty Island and Ellis Island late
last night. The Coast Guard reported difficulties in
approaching the landmarks with landing vehicles.

The refineries on the outskirts of Newark have not been on-line since a three-pronged attack by bird, fish, and forest people in early April. A reporter invited to tour the facilities found the oil storage tanks covered with rare vines. Experiments in oil reclamation use fossil fuel-eating bacteria. The old power plants are surrounded by armed police, but the police are in turn surrounded by more citizens, some in the illegal nature costumes.

Once considered an eccentric fringe element in the environmental movement, the Earthers' flocks and schools and moving forests briefly seized control of London last month. Forcing bio-systems over human social systems is not a new idea. Social observers trace influences to Alfred Hitchcock's "The Birds," and to Edward Abbey's "The Monkey Wrench Gang."

The problem, officials insist, is infiltration of teachers' unions. All the biology teachers in high schools are now held in "rubber rooms" in school buildings. Natural scientists in the universities are also reporting detentions and interrogations.

The Audubon Society and Natural Resources Defense Council insist that they have never talked to the Earthers. Bird People were photographed on the roof of the Audubon Society's headquarters in downtown New York. Infiltration of environmentalist organizations by Earthers is widely suspected by police.

Perhaps the greatest problem is what police call the "Bronx Zoo Breakout Conversions." Traffic jams are reported along the Brooklyn Queens Expressway as motorists spontaneously stop their cars and perform like animals along the highway with stereos blasting the sounds of forest birdcalls or big cat growls from the African plain. Conversions are considered the work of "wacky cults" to some, but others see the old flash mob tradition run amuck, large-scale improvisatory performances. Hundreds of vehicles have stopped in the middle of thoroughfares, with families taking bird-like positions on the roof or the hood, soaring with their arms in wing-like gestures.

Notable among the bird-performers are the police, doing the "Blue-jay Boogie," using their blue uniforms to mimic the jay. It should be noted that the Blue Jay is an aggressive bird, related to shrikes and crows, and is known for its gang-like flocking. No arrests have been reported as the BQE continues its conversion to a strange inter-species bio-highway.

APOCALYPSE
BY
TORNADO

In 1958, a muscular storm crosses into Wisconsin from Minnesota, unleashing four tornadoes, tubes of 200 mph wind leaning forward into the land of milk and butter, surprising everyone in the neat green squares of innocent Wisconsin.

To this day survivors share bad and good luck stories. A lady was milking cows and the barn flew off, and then the cows flew off too. All that was left was the milk, and it was still steaming. Stories like that.

These are F5 storms, the highest category for storm power, and they are the first F5s in Wisconsin's history. One tornado kills 28 in a single town, Colfax. Colfax is just up Highway 40 from where we lived. I was a child at the time and the spinning giants excited as much as frightened me.

I remember one summer night, a Sunday, just after Colfax. I was watching The Wonderful World of Disney with my dad. There were tornado warnings that night, and my father instructed me—"Go to the window and tell me if you see a funnel." So I ran to look out at the dark storm, and then ran back: "Nope! Not yet!"

Thinking back—how would a tornado have presented itself in the frame of that window? The screen of the television had "Night on Bald Mountain" by the drunk nobleman Modest Mussorgsky. The big bad devil mountain was pulling the Christian souls out of the cemeteries.

Thousands of skeletons and ghost-horses ride up on the wind toward the dark distant peak and a swell of ancient anguished violins and brass sense a ripple through the dead throng that flows up the clawed feet of the Devil.

Suddenly I am dispatched on another errand, this one to a second screen, our window at the front of the house, where I can see a Grant Wood-like tableau of fields, which seems to be waiting, virginally poised, for the unchristian weather. What did I think I was looking for: a black triangle on its point? Something like the sadistic giant of Bald Mountain? I run back to Dad, again and again with my report. He smiles and turns back to the TV, where the laughing dark gargoyle of a Matterhorn is throwing burning maidens over the cliff. How long did we play the game?

Just a few years later, in similar storms, I don't go to the window to watch for the unknown assailant in the dark, the marauding stranger. I go to the door and walk out to join them. Or I stay up late listening on an old yellow radio imagining the jazz flying through the static all the way from New York . . . Miles and Mingus and Coltrane. I hitch-hike down to Madison where I see Jimi Hendrix. From there, a couple escapes later, New Orleans! Chicago! And then I'm off to New York.

I fly into storms that are a lot different than Night on Bald Mountain or any other sly Disney tale, which in hindsight are so obviously just guilt-inducing-hells manufactured for consumers. When was I finally free of those? When I joined the activists and started shouting in Times Square, hurling fire and brimstone back at Mickey Mouse. Earthalujah!

Children? We didn't expect that nature would include us. We never suspected that we were THAT involved. We are actually part of the tornado? That's a complete surprise. Well, a tornado is a big surprise too, even when you know it's coming.

The media sends the union shooters into the rubble, with those hapless Eyewitness News men and women walking into the left-overs of the inferno, with their microphones out in front of them like divining rods. They are ready to rough it in Joplin or Tuscaloosa, all slick empathy, in the middle of some disaster where climate change decided to make a special visit.

Finally, the little taxpaying family walks dutifully out of their death vortex to talk to the camera. The jaunty-haired failed actor never fails to ask a cringe-inducing question like "How does it feel to have lost your home?" and the whole media ceremony supports one notion in a formal way: that the tornado was an insane monster, separate from us and not human. Definitely not good, not American. Unfeeling. Strange.

Today's Apocalypse goes like this. Congregation, this idea that nature is separate, somewhere in the background of sanctified and patriotic human life— that is an old idea that damned us from the dawn of the nature-hating gods.

The storms were supposed to be kept as a kind of guilty pleasure—separate and newsy—approximately the same thing as Al Queda or the serial killer in Long Island, as distant as the French banker with his semen stains on the hotel walls. The tornado must be a Devil only. That's all. The tornado must sell papers.

The corporations will have trouble moving on from this profitable lie: each tornado is a stand-alone tragedy. Without such mistruths those in power might find that their tabloid fodder is taking over more than the front-page. They might find that the storm won't stay put, that it's whirling into the business section, sports, style, and now the advertisements. Nothing is safe. They meddled with the REAL gods. This is an Apocalypse, not bad weather.

We are learning the hard way that we are a part of that tornado. The fact can no longer be suppressed that the same people that profit from the sale of storms as images, as tragedies, as temporary actors in a show, are also the fossil fuel-centric cause of the deadly turn of climate events. As consumers we crank up these storms, we wind them up faster and faster, they blow and blow and blow as we buy and buy and buy.

We didn't know that we were always a part of the climate. The tornadoes were never separate from us. We can portray them as evil, punishing forces or see our better selves in them. We are out there too on the plains, racing through subdivisions, lifting up the Astroturf. That's us too. Our lives echo in sky. Call it politics. Call it karma. Call it having a soul.

We are a part of the natural world. That may be hard for many of us to believe, but the storms are insisting on it. The climate comes into all the living things—because the climate is life and we are life with it. We are at the heart of the storm and the Earth feels us in its stormy heart. This might mean quick death, or an air-born ride into the next county, or revolutions of revelations. We are a part of that tornado.

Consider the old resident of tornado alley . . . the

buffalo. The humidity rising from the backs of the vast buffalo herds of the Great Plains created a "response weather." The ancient buffalo roamed with their own storms above them. Reading the journals of Lewis and Clark you might reflect on the blanketing of tornado country by warm-blooded bison, enough of them to change the wind. Let somebody say. We ARE the tornado. Let me hear you say, "Tornadoes are not Devils!"

If we stop demonizing the weather, stop separating ourselves from these extreme storms, then perhaps we'll also stop separating from the wars, from the pipelines, from the private armies surrounding the last pristine African lakes? The moment the tornadoes are not separate from us our political life changes completely.

My father probably watched the Bald Mountain Disney show for the music. He always liked big sounding symphonies like Mussorgsky. He's a Christian, and the animated skeletons and ghosts, flying up the cliffs, might have been our ancestors sleeping in the churchyards, except they didn't seem to be in heaven, as they whirled up into the sky around that devil mountain.

Father flew small planes most of his life. At the time of the Colfax tornado, he flew a yellow canvas Piper Cub, landing on flat pastures, sharing the plane with members of a local club, parking it overnight in a corrugated shed rented from a local farmer.

One time we were flying at night from Minnesota toward the Black Hills. We were up at 10,000 feet and we lost eye contact with the ground. There were storms in the area, there so often are in the Dakotas. Dad was descending as the wind picked up. He decided where we should land. I remember he talked with an air-control person and received information about wind and visibility in the form of a long string of numbers and short-hand phrases. He filed his flight plan and the voice on the radio accepted it through the static. Then suddenly it was snowing and Dad was busy looking out ahead, trying to discern the landscape, as the flurries raced through the propeller in front of us.

The dark ground came up and suddenly there was a runway, which seemed like an amazing thing to me. The wind made our landing a bumpy one. We were blown up off the tarmac once, but settled back down again. Dad's a good, patient pilot who has a feel for the wings and the wind. He smiled when we pulled up to the hangar. He didn't ever admit that we were in danger.

I could not help noticing, however, that he had a very concerned look on his face. The hangar and little airport building were unfamiliar to him. We tied down the plane and walked through the blowing snow toward the light in the window. We walked up to a big bald guy at the counter. He told us we had landed in the wrong town. "You're welcome to wait out the storm here!" he said "Or there's a motel down highway 20, over near Dupree. I'm sure they got some beds."

SANDY STOPS OUR SHOPPING

One last thing—
here on the eve of
Black Friday, 2012

After our talk with Pam, I carry Lena up the stoop and she joins Savi inside. Then I walk over to the park, stepping over the downed branches.

As I approach the forest, I can't help but remember the scary gusts of the hurricane, all the horizontal flying things. Have I experienced anything like this before? Once I was in a boat that exploded. Such a moment tears the names off of objects, rips the feelings from ideas . . . Sandy might be just what we needed.

As I cross into the greenery of Prospect Park, I hear deep growling sounds. 50,000 lb. debris removal trucks are everywhere, sitting there idling. I walk up the hill where George Washington watched the Brits kill the Marylanders in the Battle of Brooklyn. A city block up the hill the exhaust from the line of trucks smells up the place, flooding the woods.

So the trucks full of dead and dying trees are cleaning up after Sandy while continuing to burn the fossil fuels that caused Sandy. Well . . .

The title of this book is the old phrase, The End of the World. If we have that experience together, then it is a crushing encounter with RIGHT NOW. If we are all of us drawing our last breath together, if we press against the unknown together, we are in the classic "I want to live" moment. And we have the courage to do the necessary act, regardless of its foolishness. We're at that point now.

Do we still think that The End of the World has a six second delay that will re-engineer our screams into sexy giggles? No, The End of the World insists that we stop shopping, stop banking, stop bombing—stop living in those little squares of time and space that make Consumerism run. The End of the World is giving us a few more minutes to confront the manufacturers of this over-arching con-job, the big bankers and CEOs. Can we run up to their corner offices and pull them from their speaker-phones and computers?

Up in the woods of the park, I'm picking my way forward in the late twilight, and I find a hickory tree. I'm standing there in the soft, swirly wind that is down inside the forest, the damp smells of evening coming up, my feet on the matted forest floor. It's early night. It's the shift-change from hawks to owls, from white-throated sparrows to chimney swifts and night herons.

In the darkening trees—just standing here I feel like I'm praying. I know this is my church. And I know that this moment now can be carried with the Stop Shopping Gospel Choir into a cocktail party or a bank lobby or the Senate cafeteria and remain intact, the main faith.

In this book I've shared my personal work at making an Earthy religion. The miraculous childhood stories mix with the activism that changed my life. The ecosystems that set me to dreaming, forests and the plains east of the Black Hills mixes with my family and my city. Doesn't each of us have this job? . . . to find our crucial ties with Earth and report them.

And what is post-fundamentalist religion, after all? Without the structure inherited from professional priests, rabbis, imams, CEOs, and the herd of celebrity spokespersons—we have the brew of our own lives, which we raise to stories and songs and rituals out of respect for Earth that created us.

Life is an unexplained miracle. This impossible world is what we have to work with, to enjoy—to have and then leave. This impossible life is the source of our insistence on the possible. The more amazed we are by the gift of life, the easier it is to defend it. This life makes us unafraid to pull the bankers from their

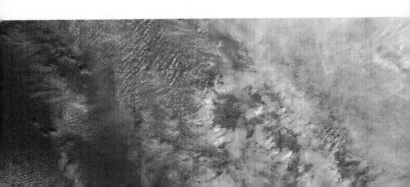

computers, to take them back to the forest for a lesson in living.

I have to be careful walking—there are trees down everywhere. The hurricane blew down or snapped and twisted to stumps more than a thousand trees in this great urban park. Sandy was just here. While we got a big storm, Europe got a big strike. The streets of Madrid and Athens and so many European cities were overflowing with citizens re-claiming their governments. The crowds look like ocean surges, like great intentional storms. There is Climate Change powering our Social Change!

I stand in a forest, where the consequences of our poisons are jaggedly all around me, and think these long thoughts of activism. But I know that love is the instruction we get from Earth. We know that violence makes Climate Change, and we can't see how violence would end it.

We stand at the front door of Macy's as the police open the demonstration pen fence and Macy's carefully opens its door from the inside at Thanksgiving midnight, the doorbuster moment.

We have our backs at the door. We face thousands of Consumers surging toward us, their faces like pumped up balloons.

WE ARE THE EARTH RIOTS!

WE ARE RESPONSIBLE CITIZENS!

SANDY SAYS STOP YOUR SHOPPING!

YOU DON'T HAVE TO BUY A GIFT TO GIVE
A GIFT!

WE'RE TREE PEOPLE!

WE'RE BIRD PEOPLE!

STOP SHOPPING!

WE'RE MOUNTAINS!

WE'RE WETLANDS!

WE'RE THE STORM!

SANDY SAYS STOP SHOPPING!

JOIN AN ECOSYSTEM AND SAVE YOURSELF!

BLACK FRIDAY IS THE END OF THE WORLD!

STOP SHOPPING START LIVING!

We are carried into the foray by the consumers and we don't go down fighting. We go down
loving—
to the END!

This
Turning
World

When we're wondering what to do
Apocalypses come right through
The flames are high, the floods are too
From this world I thought I knew
This natural world that brought
me you

Fires, floods, tsunamis, quakes
What a difference
Apocalypse makes

When we're wondering where to turn
Apocalypses make us learn
The sky it burns, the blackbirds cry
In this world where I will die
This natural world—we all must die

Fires, floods, tsunamis, quakes
What a difference
Apocalypse makes

ACKNOWLEDGMENTS

I gratefully acknowledge the person who edited this book, Savitri D. Our friend Jonathan Ellis published the book, patiently steering me through the minutia of things like ISBN numbers. Charles Gaines, Eric Drooker, Urania Mylonas, Harry Ram, Savitri D, and Nate Schneider from Waging Nonviolence were generous readers and editors. Thanks to visual collaborator Courtney Andujar, and as ever to my book agent William Clark.

Joel Kovel, at the Eco Socialist, Ben Dubin-Thaler, founder of the Biobus, and forestry scientist and otter lover Melissa Savage all answered my calls as I pursued scientific answers to anxious questions.

Burner, lawyer, and friend Wylie Stecklow sprung us from jail time after time and Maggie Best nourished us with meals and gentle wisdom.

Thanks to Steve McMaster, Matthew Roth, Christabel Gough, Aaron Sosnick, and Marion R. Weber of The Arts & Healing Network for their enduring support through this time, as Lena Nightstar learned to walk and talk.

As ever my deepest gratitude to the radical warblers of the Stop Shopping Choir, with a nod especially to Gaylen Hamilton and his loyal partner Johnny Cash.

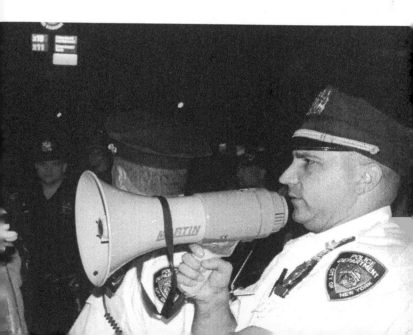

IMAGE CREDITS

6-7: Hurricane Sandy, October 26, 2012. NASA, MODIS/ LANCE, HDF File Data processed by Supportstorm / Michon Scott.

8-9: FEMA / NOAA News Photo.

10-11: Reverend Billy. John Quilty.

12: Smartphone. Clahote; Skulls, Fontanelle Cemetery. Augusto De Luca.

15: Empty supermarket shelves before Hurricane Sandy, Montgomery, NY. Daniel Case.

16: Rinjani, 1994. CC-BY-2.0, GFDL.

17: Decoration from the end of Book 2, Section 1 in Andrew Motte's 1729 translation of Newton's The Mathematical Principles of Natural Philosophy.

20: Atomic cloud over Hiroshima. NARA 542192 / Enola Gay Tail Gunner S/Sgt. George R. (Bob) Caron.

22-23: NASA mission AS17, roll 148, frame 22727.

26: Bomb and blast damage to Hallam Street and Duchess Street during the Blitz, Westminster, London, 1940. City of Westminster Archives Centre.

28: Pyramid with the all-seeing eye on the back of a US dollar bill.

36-37: Hororary medal of the Hanseatic City of Lübeck / Adolph von Menzel; Painting of Prospect Park, Brooklyn, 1910 / Paul Sawyier.

42-43: Forest ceiling. Jason Pratt.

44-45: FEMA / NOAA News Photo.

46: Tree on an overcast day. Terry Korte.

54-55: Horse's eye. Wikimedia Commons / Kallerna.

56-57: Typhoon in Hong Kong. Wikimedia Commons / Mcyjerry.

58: Dance of Death woodcut, 1493. Michael Wolgemut.

61: Artwork by Banksy, Bristol, England. Photograph by Adrian Pingstone.

65: Jail hallway in the Petropavlovsk fortress, St. Petersburg, Russia. Wikimedia Commons / Pöllö.

66-67: Apokalipsa, oil on canvas, 1854. Ignacy Gierdziejewski.

68: Slice of pumpkin pie. Wikimedia Commons / Evan-Amos.

72-73: FEMA / NOAA News Photo.

74: Mountains. Guilhem Vellut.

82: Oklahoma, May 4, 1999. Andrea Booher / FEMA News Photo.

88-89: Line art representation of a swift. Pearson Scott Foresman.

93: Sparks on dark water. Wikimedia Commons / Vassil.

94-95: FEMA / NOAA News Photo.

104-105: New York skyline during a blackout due to a power failure during Hurricane Sandy. David Shankbone.

111: The Stop Shopping Gospel Choir. Brennan Cavanaugh.

112-113: Hurricane Sandy in New York City, October 29, 2012. Jordan Balderas.

114: An etching by Jan Luyken from the Phillip Medhurst Collection of Bible illustrations housed at Belgrave Hall, Leicester, England (The Kevin Victor Freestone Bequest). Photograph by Philip De Vere.

116-117: Reverend Billy with cop and bull horn. Brandon O'Neill.